TIPS FOR NEW BRIDES

Tiptionary Journals

are a unique concept that combine selected tips from the best-selling book, Tiptionary™, with space to write down all of those tips, shortcuts and ideas that have either been handed down to you from family and friends, or that you have discovered through "trial and error" along the way.

Tips for the New Bride takes

a practical approach to offering helpful advice, by including only those tips that would be applicable to a married couple. We know that not every tip offered will be acted upon, nor should it be, but what we do offer is the opportunity to learn that there are many different ways to accomplish goals, cheaply and efficiently. When there's more than one way to achieve the same result, the tips you will find in this volume will help you make that choice.

TIPS HERE:

The useful and practical tips you'll find in Tips for the New Bride, combined with your own ideas and insights will provide a valuable reference tool that will be used again and again, for years to come. And who knows? This may be the book that your children use later in their life when they want to find out, "How did Mom do that?"

The best thing about good advice is, it never goes out of style.

CLOTHING

Button security

Buttons on new clothes often fall off after just one wearing and washing. Before you wear a new item, cover the thread on each button with clear nail polish or a drop of Super Glue™. Just be careful not to get any on the fabric.

Clothing swap

Arrange a clothing swap with friends. Ask everyone to bring at least five items in good condition that no longer fit, flatter, or meet their needs. One person's disaster could be your delight.

Static cling

Annoyed by static cling? Massage a small amount of hand lotion into your hands. Then lightly rub your palms over your panty hose, tights, or slip.

OTHER TIPS

OTHER TIPS

Swimsuits

To prolong the life of swimsuits that are exposed to harsh chlorine, buy a bottle of chlorine remover, sold in pet supply stores for removing chlorine from the water in fish tanks. Add a few drops of the liquid to a pail of cold water, pop the suits in when you are done swimming, and follow with a cold tap water rinse.

Ink stains

Aerosol hairsprays, because they contain a high concentration of acetone, will remove some ballpoint ink stains from clothing. Try this: Hold a rag under the fabric to blot the ink that comes through on the other side, then aim and spray. Remember this tip when you're at the office and get an ink stain. Someone will usually have hairspray and the key to beating an ink stain is to get at it as quickly as possible.

Collar and cuff turn

Save money on men's dress shirts. If the collar or cuffs wear out first, take the shirt to a dry cleaner or tailor (or learn to do it yourself) and have them turned. It will cost about $5.00 to $10.00, which of course is much less than the cost of a new shirt.

Classic is timeless

Buying classic clothing is a money saver. What's "in" today looks ridiculous tomorrow. Buy timeless, simple clothes, maintain one weight, and you will reduce your clothing expenditures. Classic pieces for the wardrobe all tend to work together too.

Zipper jams

Paint those fraying threads that constantly get caught in a zipper with clear nail polish.

Fraying collars

Use an old electric razor to "shave" the collars of men's cotton oxford dress shirts when they begin to pill. Men's neck whiskers chew up collars, and the "shaving" actually helps to slow the wearing out process. They come out looking like new, literally.

OTHER TIPS

OTHER TIPS

Dry-clean only

Think twice or three times before deciding to buy something that says, "dry-clean only." This kind of expensive maintenance will double or even triple the cost of a garment over the years.

Debit merchandise

Make friends with the managers of your favorite stores, and you might be able to tap into a gold mine. Ask if their "debits" or used merchandise are available for sale. These are the items that have been returned for one reason or another but cannot be put back on the floor or returned to the manufacturer. Typically these items are sold for pennies on the dollar.

Hangers affect fabrics

Don't store clothing on wooden hangers. Over time, the acid in the wood can react with the fabric. Wire hangers aren't much better. Pad all nonplastic hangers with unbleached muslin or cotton.

Wholesale

As a general rule, don't pay full price. With so many manufacturer outlets, discount mail-order catalogs, consignment shops, thrift shops, and fabulous sales, you should never have to pay the full retail price for your clothing or shoes.

Zipper troubles

There are several things you can do to get that stubborn, sluggish, sticking metal zipper back into tip-top shape: Run the lead of an ordinary pencil along the metal zipper teeth to lubricate them. Or, with a cotton swab, apply a bit of lubricating spray such as WD-40™ to the teeth. Be careful to wipe away any excess so it won't soil the garment. Another solution: Rub the edge of a bar of soap or an old candle up and down the teeth and along both sides of the zipper.

OTHER TIPS

OTHER TIPS

ENTERTAINMENT

Cheap movies

Go to a movie matinee. It's always cheaper.

Cheap tickets

If you enjoy cultural events or visiting local museums and theaters, volunteer as an usher or ticket collector or to fill some other need. In exchange you will probably receive free or reduced admissions. Ask about the policy ahead of time.

Go to college

Local colleges often show movies in a setting that's better than some small theaters and at a much lower cost.

Free concerts

Most cities have community sponsored entertainment during summer months. Many churches and colleges have free performances during holidays. Make it a habit to check the paper and community bulletin board for local events.

Interlibrary loans

Call your library to see if you can borrow that book you've been tempted to buy. If they don't have it on hand, ask for an interlibrary loan. Even small libraries belong to large networks of libraries, and chances are very good they'll be able to get that book for you and in less time than it would take for them to go through the channels necessary to acquire it for their own shelves.

Rehearsals

If tickets to a special concert or local play are out of your price range, inquire if you can attend a rehearsal.

Skip first-run films

All but the biggest blockbusters are available on video three months after release. Your patience will pay off.

OTHER TIPS

OTHER TIPS

Progressive party

Instead of everyone in your circle of friends hosting a separate holiday party, make plans to have a progressive dinner. The dinner party moves from one house to another, starting with cocktails and hors d'oeuvres at the first stop, appetizer or soup at the second, main course at the next, and dessert and coffee at the last. It's an enjoyable way to share the burden and the glory, and you get to see everyone's holiday decorations too.

Mealtime fun

Make eating at home fun. Rearrange your eating area. Make a new tablecloth. Use place mats. Play background music. Light some candles. Have a picnic in your family room.

Mirror notes

Leave a reminder for family members by writing notes on the bathroom mirror with a dry erase marker, available in all kinds of colors at office supply stores. It wipes right off with a tissue, and it's sure to be seen. If a note is left unerased for some time, use a bit of rubbing alcohol on that tissue to wipe it away without a trace.

Stargaze

Get a book about constellations from the library and arrange a starry night outing to identify constellations. Bring a thermos of hot chocolate and a great big, cozy blanket.

GIFTS

Mall alternatives

You can either shop at trendy mall stores for gift items like scented soaps, bath sponges, bath beads, etc., to give as gifts (and spend a "s"mall fortune) or you can find reasonable facsimile products, often the exact same thing, at discount stores like Wal-Mart, where two bars of scented soap are $2.38 and a "squishy" or sponge is about $2.00.

OTHER TIPS

OTHER TIPS

Everything gifts

One couple we know has begun giving an "everything" present to each other for the entire year's gifts (birthday, anniversary, Christmas, etc.) One year their everything gift was a new computer; once it was a piece of home gym equipment a physical therapist had recommended. Not only does it free their time, they say they are not purchasing items they neither need nor want, just to be buying a gift. The fringe benefit they have noticed is the money they now have available at Christmastime and throughout the year to help those less fortunate than themselves.

Gift cards

Make your holiday card the gift. Include a family picture, poem, story, original song, or painting— anything of lasting significance.

IOU's

IOU gifts are often the most valuable and appreciated of all. Make up a coupon that is redeemable for something you do well, and tuck it inside a meaningful card. Give what you do best, and you will have given the best gift of all.

Valentine, Nebraska

Want to really impress your sweetheart? Have your valentine arrive with a postmark from Valentine, Nebraska. It's easy: Prepare your valentine, address and stamp the envelope. Put it into a larger envelope. Address it to Postmaster, Valentine, NE 69201-9998, and mail it off. Enclose a brief note asking that they postmark and send off your valentine to arrive on or before February 14.

Books

Books make great gifts. But don't limit yourself to shopping in the big bookstore chains. Secondhand bookstores are less expensive and often have out-of-print titles that can't be found in the big chains. Also these stores may sell old prints or maps that you could frame for your family members or friends.

OTHER TIPS

OTHER TIPS

Create gift stationery

You can avoid spending if you get into the habit of making your own cards, stationery, postcards, gift bags, etc. You can purchase paper and envelopes in bulk then us the paper cutter at the local copy shop to cut it to the sizes you need. With a few carefully chosen rubber stamps and colored markers, anyone can make beautiful and unique cards and stationery for personal use or to give as gifts. Use postcards when-ever possible. This way you'll not only save the cost of the envelope, but 13 cents in postage too.

Gift list

Avoid returning unwanted gifts (or pretending you like them) from your spouse or immediate family members by keeping an ongoing record of the things you would like, along with the specific details. Through the year as you see items of particular interest, pick up the store's business card and on the back write the details such as: Red cardigan sweater, brass buttons, wool blend, size eight, $49.98. These cards become a practical gift list that makes gift giving a positive experience for both the giver and receiver.

Gifts of food

Personalize food gifts with your
own decorated label, for example,
"Marilyn's Chutney" or "Cathy's
Cookies." Attach your recipe and
other instructions to the gift with
ribbon, raffia, or tasseled cord. Add
a spoon or spreader for chutneys or
flavored butters.

Gift stash

Create a gift box in a closet or
cupboard into which you can put
any free samples you receive, door
prizes you win, and gifts you don't
like but somebody else might.
Always be on the lookout for things
to add to your box. When you need
a present in a hurry or don't have the
cash to spend, go directly to the gift
box, and chances are you'll find just
the right thing.

Reusable gift containers

Cover gift boxes with appliques,
needlework, and quilts, or
embroider the recipient's name.
These kinds of containers are
especially appreciated because they
become part of the gift itself. Wrap
the box and the lid separately, and
the gift box becomes an heirloom to
be cherished for years to come.

OTHER TIPS

OTHER TIPS

Flowers direct

Before you call a local florist or a national floral delivery company to arrange for an out-of-area delivery, think about this: These services end up involving all kinds of middlemen, which means extra fees and surcharges for phone calls and delivery. They usually have minimums of about $40.00, and you're never sure what your recipient will get because you don't come close to speaking with the person who will actually create the arrangement. You can skip past all of these extra people by making one call to a florist in the neighborhood where your recipient lives. You'll get three times the bouquet and service for your money by dealing directly.

HEALTH AND BEAUTY

OTHER TIPS

Blush correctly

To find the right blush, check the color of your skin after exercising and try to match that color. Blush should add a healthy glow, not introduce a foreign color.

Buff nails

Buff your fingernails rather than polish them because it's a quicker and cheaper way to groom nails. Apply a bit of petroleum jelly as a buffing compound, which will also soften cuticles.

Cosmetics, economy line

If you love a particular high-priced cosmetic line, inquire as to the name of their economy line. For example, Lancome™ (available in department stores) also produces the L'Oreal™ line (available in any drugstore). You can call the customer service department of your favorite line to inquire.

OTHER TIPS

Foot massage

Give your tired feet a mini massage by rolling them back and forth over an icy cold soda or juice can.

Elbows

Elbows get lots of wear and tear, and they really show it. Here's the perfect way to give them the attention they deserve: Cut a lemon in half and rest an elbow in each section for at least 10 minutes. The lemon juice will actually remove the stains that make elbows look dirty.

Eye makeup remover

Use a no-tears type baby shampoo to remove eye makeup. Ophthalmologists encourage contact lens wearers to do this to reduce protein buildup on their lenses. Apply with a cotton swab in a brushing motion while holding eyelid taut. Rinse thoroughly.

Makeup remover

Use baby wipes to remove makeup.
They're made for sensitive skins
and won't cause dryness or
irritation.

Health clubs

Try the club before you join. Most
offer several free visits or short, low
cost trial memberships. Join with a
group of five or so friends, and at
some clubs you'll save as much as
35 percent. Pay a year's dues in
advance and save up to 20 percent
(make sure the club has a reasonable
likelihood of still being in business
a year from now). Ask about new
member perquisites, such as a free
session with a personal trainer.
Also, if you need to take a long-
term break for travel or other
reasons, ask the club to freeze your
membership and start it up again
upon return.

Petroleum jelly

Apply a small amount of petroleum
jelly to your skin nightly. It's a
natural moisturizer and is especially
effective on extra dry areas like
elbows, heels, and knees.

OTHER TIPS

OTHER TIPS

Sunless tan

Smooth baby oil onto skin and allow it to penetrate before applying sunless tanning lotions to achieve a more even, lighter tanning effect, especially on elbows and feet.

Tired feet

Freshen tired feet and soften skin easily and quickly. Add four tablespoons of baking soda to one quart of warm water. Pour into a large container, and let your footsies soak in it for 10 minutes.

Herbal bath

There's nothing like a relaxing, naturally scented bath to revive a tired mind and body. Fill a piece of cheesecloth with fresh rosemary, tie it up with string, hang the bag from the faucet, and fill the tub.

Take vitamin C

Vitamin C works in the body as a scavenger, picking up all sorts of trash, including virus trash. It can shorten the length of a cold from seven days to maybe two or three. It has been proven to lower cholesterol, decrease arthritis pain, reduce outbreaks of canker sores, and lessen premenstrual syndrome.

Cologne

Refrigerate your cologne, and it can last up to two years. If a fragrance is exposed to heat, air, or sunlight, it immediately begins to change.

Exfoliant

Mix 1/2 to 2/3 cup granulated sugar with the juice of one whole lemon to form a paste. While showering, invigorate your skin with the paste. Rub heels and elbows with the inside of the lemon rinds. This costs 12 cents per treatment. A comparable brand-name product costs $25.00 for a four-ounce jar.

Nail fix

Tea bag paper can mend a broken nail instantly and easily. First cut paper to fit the nail, then coat with clear nail polish.

OTHER TIPS

OTHER TIPS

Nail polish prep

Scrub your fingernails with white vinegar, rinse, and dry completely. Now apply your nail polish. It will adhere better and last longer.

Face-lift

Here's how to give yourself an instant "face-lift" and beauty treatment: Mix one teaspoon each of baking soda and olive oil to form a slightly thick paste. Gently massage it into your skin, rinse well and then pat dry.

Hairspray clogs

Ordinary rubbing alcohol will unclog the spray nozzle of a hairspray container that even hot water has not been able to unclog. Just dip the nozzle into the rubbing alcohol, allow to sit for a few minutes, wipe off, and spray.

Shampoo

Don't be a shampoo snob. In a 1992 Consumer Reports test of 132 brand-name shampoos, the lowly cheap brands from the supermarket rated just as high as the pricey salon brands.

Visit the men's department

Buy men's toiletries if you have a choice when it comes to unscented deodorant, shaving foam, and hair colorings, for example. Products manufactured specifically for men are significantly cheaper ounce for ounce. Go figure.

Hair control

The combination of lemon, which closes the hair cuticle, and lime, which is slightly emollient, helps break up static electricity and puts an end to flyaway hair. Mix one teaspoon lemon juice, 1/2 teaspoon lime juice, and one cup of water. Mix together and pour into a plastic spray bottle. Spritz onto clean, damp hair. Do not rinse. Style as usual. Keeps well up to five days in the refrigerator.

Cash discount

Whenever undergoing a dental or medical procedure for which you will eventually pay, inquire about a cash discount. Do not be timid about expecting as much as 25 percent discount when you pay by check or cash at the time the procedure is done. Never be afraid to ask.

OTHER TIPS

OTHER TIPS

Hair residue remover

Mix one tablespoon dry baking soda with the amount of shampoo you normally use for one hair washing, and shampoo your hair with the mixture. This removes residue buildup and leaves hair shiny and bouncy. Repeat about once a month. This is a cheap substitute for very expensive commercial products that do the very same thing.

Skin care products

A reader asked a doctor friend what he learned during his dermatology rotation concerning expensive skin and facial cleansing products. He informed her that the best products are not the most expensive. Dermatologists recommend Dove™ or Lever 2000™ for cleansing and Lubriderm™ lotion for moisturizing. Both products are sold over the counter at any drug and most grocery stores.

Generic equivalents

Ask for generic prescriptions, which cost up to 50 percent less, yet by law must have the same chemical makeup and potency. Also, buy generic non-prescription pain medication. Advil™ costs about $8.00 for 100 tablets, while ibuprofen (the active ingredient in Advil™) costs about $2.00 for the same amount. The same goes for Tylenol™. It is acetaminophen. Drug companies take advantage of the naive public and try to get them to believe that aspirin works so much better if it costs twice the price and has a brand-name. Consult the pharmacist when in doubt.

Hospital bills

Carefully examine hospital bills even if you have full insurance coverage. If you go in for a knee reconstruction and are billed for infant nursery time, put up a fuss. Hospitals are notorious for making these kinds of mistakes, and a good consumer scrutinizes every charge. Report all discrepancies to the hospital, physician, and insurance company.

OTHER TIPS

OTHER TIPS

Physician samples

Every doctor's office is flooded with all kinds of expensive prescription samples, also known as "stock bottles" When required to take a medication, be sure to ask your doctor if he or she might have samples for you to try. Asking for sufficient samples to make sure the medication is right for you is especially wise, particularly if you might be allergic to it. Don't hesitate to ask again every time you come to the office. Doctors can even write a prescription for a stock bottle to be filled at the pharmacy for patients unable to afford the prescription.

Split those tablets

If you doctor prescribes, for example, 50 mg dosage tablets, ask about changing that to the 100 mg version so you can break the tablets in two to accomplish the 50 mg dosage. If this is possible, you will save a lot of money because the difference in price between 100 mg and 50 mg will usually be negligible. You can purchase a tablet splitter for just a few dollars at any pharmacy. Caution: Some pills' delivery systems may be affected by splitting them in half. Check with your doctor or pharmacist first.

BAKING

OTHER TIPS

Baking location

Bake pies, tarts, and quiches in the lower third of the oven. The bottom crust will be crisp, and the rim or top crust won't over-brown.

Baking multiples

When baking more than one item at a time, make sure there's plenty of room between the pans, walls, and racks of the oven for air to circulate.

Brownies

For extra-fudgy brownies, add one tablespoon corn syrup to the batter, either a box mix or from scratch. Bake as usual. Also, don't assume it always pays to bake from scratch. Brownies, for example, are often cheaper to make from a mix.

Cake cooling

To cool a cake that has just come out of the oven, place the pan on a wet towel. The cake is less likely to stick to the pan if it's cooled this way.

OTHER TIPS

Cake decorator

A clean, squeezable mustard bottle is great for decorating cakes. Just fill it with the color you want, screw on the pointed tip, and get to work on that cake.

Cake writing like a pro

Use a toothpick to sketch letters onto a frosted cake before you try to write "Happy Birthday" or another message with icing. If you make a mistake, smooth the top and start again. When you're happy with your lettering, simply apply icing along the sketched lines.

Heart-shaped cake

No special pan is required for this cake. Using your favorite recipe or box mix, bake one round layer and one square layer, cool and remove from pans. On a large tray, platter, or foil covered cardboard, place the square layer with corners pointing up, down, right, and left so it looks like a diamond. Slice the round layer into two equal halves. Place a half on two adjacent sides of the square layer. Frost and decorate as desired.

Cookies

A thin coat of nonstick vegetable spray on cookie cutters will prevent dough from sticking to the metal. This also works with your children's play dough. You can also put a slice of bread in the cookie jar to absorb the moisture that causes cookies to become stale.

Cupcakes

To keep plastic wrap from sticking to cupcakes (and other homemade frosted treats), spray the plastic wrap with some nonstick cooking spray. The cupcakes will arrive at their destination with frosting intact.

OTHER TIPS

OTHER TIPS

Don't peek

Don't peek into the oven when you are baking something. Each peek can cost as much as 25 degrees, will affect the baking quality, and you won't know when it's truly finished baking. Watch the timer instead.

Hot rolls

To keep dinner rolls hot at the table, heat a ceramic tile in the oven while the rolls are baking. Put the warm tile in a bread basket, cover it with a napkin, and lay the rolls on top. Cover the rolls with a napkin, too, and they'll stay warm for the entire meal.

Low-fat trick

When baking, you can cut down on or omit the amount of butter or margarine used by substituting applesauce. A good rule of thumb is no more than one tablespoon of applesauce per one cup of flour.

Cookie sheets

If you have trouble with cookies burning in your oven, place a second cookie sheet under the first one before baking.

Bread dough rising

To create the perfect environment for bread rising, bring two cups of water to a boil in a two-quart pot. Remove the pot from the heat, invert the pot's lid on the top of the pot, and lay a potholder on the inverted lid. Put the dough in a mixing bowl, balance the bowl on the inverted lid, and cover with a dishtowel. The water releases its heat gradually and keeps the dough at an ideal proofing temperature.

Piecrust

To prevent piecrust edges from over-browning, cut the bottom and sides from a disposable aluminum foil pie pan, leaving the rim intact. When the crust is light golden brown and the filling isn't quite done, place the foil ring on top to slow the browning process. The foil rim can be used again and again.

OTHER TIPS

OTHER TIPS

Spaghetti anchors

To keep the layers from slipping while you ice the sides of a layer cake, push three long sticks of dry spaghetti down through all of the layers of the cake. Frost the sides and top and pull the spaghetti out once the icing has set.

Springform pan

To easily remove a cake from the base of a springform pan, grease the base well before adding the batter or pastry. When the baked cake has cooled, place the springform pan over a hot burner for a few seconds, moving it over the burner to heat the entire bottom slightly. You may hear a pop as the cake is released. Remove pan from heat, release and remove pan sides, then slide the cake onto a serving plate.

Icing cakes

To prevent frosting drippings and smears on the cake plate, slip several strips of waxed paper just slightly under the edge of the cake all the way around. Once the frosting is set, gently remove the paper to reveal the clean platter.

Measuring cup

Dust your measuring cup with flour before measuring out molasses or honey for your next cookie recipe. The molasses or honey will pour out of the cup easily, and clean up will be a snap.

Timing

When you put a cake, pie, or bread in the oven, write down the time. That way, if anything goes wrong with the timer you won't be stuck guessing.

CULINARY TRICKS

Bargains

Search for bargains in the day-old baked goods, dented can, and meat that is about to expire bins. You have to be careful, but as long as the cans are not bulging or leaking and the appearance and dates meet your approval, go for it. Also look for generic and off-brands for additional savings.

Snacks

Keep marshmallows, potato chips, pretzels, and crackers in the freezer. They are best if frozen in their original unopened containers.

OTHER TIPS

OTHER TIPS

Dairy

The date on dairy products is the date when retailers must pull unsold products from the shelf. Properly stored, the product will be good for at least seven days past the printed date.

Punch cubes

Freeze whatever drink you are serving in an ice cube tray ahead of time. If serving tea, make tea cubes; if punch, punch cubes. Drinks will stay chilled and won't get all watered down.

Discontinued products

Today's grocery stores will only carry those items that move well in order to maintain their profit margin. Watch for product shelf labels with either a line drawn through the price code numbers or the letters "DC" or "Discontinued" written on them. By purchasing these "unadvertised" specials, you will often find savings of at least 20 percent or more on your register tape.

Skinless

To remove skin from uncooked poultry, grasp it with a paper towel and pull.

Generic

Some generic grocery items are exactly the same as the more expensive brand-name version. By law, certain items, such as aspirin, baking soda, cornstarch, honey, molasses, peanuts, pecans, salt, sugar, unbleached flour, and walnuts must be exactly the same content and composition, regardless of packaging or quantity gimmicks. Always buy the lower cost generic brands when buying these items.

Ground meat

The plastic bags that come out of cereal boxes can be used for freezing ground meat. Place the meat in the bag and flatten it out as much as the bag allows. After it freezes the ground meat can be stored on end in a vertical position, taking up very little freezer space. It also thaws more quickly.

OTHER TIPS

OTHER TIPS

Marinade

Once the meat has been removed from a marinade, the marinade can be used for a dipping sauce or saved for future use, provided you first boil it for a full three minutes to destroy any bacteria left behind by the raw meat or poultry.

Nuts

Buy walnuts, almonds, pecans, and other nuts after the holidays at sale prices. Shell, then store the nuts in individual plastic bags in the freezer. The nuts won't stick together, so it's easy to remove only what you need for each recipe.

Use before

Never purchase more meat than you can properly refrigerate and reasonably use within the following periods of time: Ground beef and beef cut into small pieces, such as stew meat, should be used within two days of purchase. Steak should be used within four days of purchase, and roast should be used within one week. If you cannot comply, be sure to freeze as soon as possible.

Popcorn

Keep popcorn kernels in the freezer. They will stay fresh much longer, and freezing will encourage every kernel to pop.

One pound equivalents

The following amounts are equal to one pound: 2 cups butter; 2 1/3 cups white granulated sugar; 2 cups packed brown sugar; 2 3/4 cups confectioners' sugar; 3 1/2 cups all-purpose flour; 4 cups cake flour; 3 3/4 cups whole wheat flour; 4 cups cocoa; 3 cups loosely packed raisins; 2 3/4 cups sliced apples; 2 cups fresh pitted cherries; 5 cups sliced, fresh mushrooms; 3 cups sliced white potatoes; 4 1/2 cups coarsely sliced cabbage

Turkey

Cooked poultry, especially turkey, can dry out very quickly. To save your guests the ordeal of a dry meal, slice the turkey and arrange on a heat-proof platter. Prepare a sauce of half butter and half chicken broth. Pour it on sliced bird, and let it stand in a 250 degree oven for 10 minutes to soak up the juices.

OTHER TIPS

OTHER TIPS

Batter

A spill-proof way to pour cupcake batter into muffin tins or pancake batter onto a griddle is to transfer it first to a clean, waxed milk carton, using a funnel. The carton's spout lets you pour with precision and provides an excellent closable container for storage in the refrigerator.

Pasta stretch

To receive more value from prepackaged pasta dishes such as Kraft Macaroni and Cheese™ or Hamburger Helper™, add up to a cup of extra macaroni or pasta to extend the dish without losing flavor. There is still plenty of sauce for the extra macaroni. To save on calories and fat, use skim milk and half the recommended amount of butter.

Sugar

Freezing brown and powdered sugars will prevent lumps.

Quick cooking

Think of the donut shape when you need to save cooking time. Foods cook slowest in the center. By eliminating the center area, all portions of the food will receive the most energy and will cook faster and more evenly.

Soup

The general rule is that soups should be cooked in a covered pot to facilitate the retention of nutrients and flavor. However, when a very thin soup needs to reduce, the pot should be only partially covered to allow for evaporation of the water and to intensify the flavors.

Egg whites

Separate whites from yolks as soon as you remove eggs from the refrigerator. Cold yolks are firmer and less likely to break. Do not pierce yolks. One speck will keep whites from beating properly. To get the greatest volume, bring eggs to room temperature before beating. Use a small, deep bowl so beaters are immersed and mixture is thoroughly aerated.

OTHER TIPS

OTHER TIPS

Frozen whipped cream

Fill a waxed milk carton with whipped cream and freeze. When you need some, cut the required amount off the top with a carving knife (carton and all). Recap the carton with plastic wrap or foil, secure with tape or a rubber band, and return to the freezer.

Pick a fish

For best quality, buy from supermarkets that display fish on ice in refrigerator cases. A fresh caught fish has almost no odor; it will not smell "fishy" An ammonia-like smell develops when fish has been stored several days-don't buy! The eyes should look clear, not cloudy; the scales should be bright pink (not gray). The flesh should be unblemished, edges intact (not torn); when pressed with a finger, the flesh should give slightly but bounce back.

Jam

To serve jelly or jam, transfer it to a squeeze bottle like a mustard bottle. Snip the end of the tip to make a slightly larger hole. No more messy jars.

Brown Sugar

One cup of granulated sugar is an adequate substitute for one cup of packed brown sugar.

Honey

One cup of honey can be replaced with 1 1/4 cups sugar and an additional 1/4 cup of whatever liquid is used in the recipe.

Fruit juice

Stretch concentrated fruit juice. Add more water than instructions recommend. You will be pleasantly surprised when you detect little difference, if any. Start by adding one half of a can of water extra. Eventually work up to one full can of water beyond the amount recommended. This will cut your concentrated fruit juice bill by 25 percent.

OTHER TIPS

OTHER TIPS

FRUITS AND VEGETABLES

Bananas
If you keep bananas in a closed plastic bag, they will keep at least two weeks on your counter.

Cauliflower
To keep cauliflower white while cooking, add a little milk to the water.

Citrus spray
Fill a spray bottle with lemon-lime soft drink to spray on apple and banana slices to prevent them from turning brown.

Corn
Keep it cool. Don't pack fresh corn on the cob in a hot trunk after you leave the store. Be sure to put it in the refrigerator immediately when you get home. To get the silk off the corn quickly, put on a pair of rubber gloves and rub the cob. The silk will come off easily. When boiling corn, add sugar to the water instead of salt. Salt will toughen the corn.

Fruit bowls

Garnish fruit bowls with fresh basil, which repels fruit flies.

Onion peeling

Peel onions under cold running water, then freeze them for five minutes before chopping or slicing them. This will keep you from crying while working with them.

Ripening

Tomatoes, avocados, peaches, and nectarines ripen faster when enclosed in a brown paper bag and kept at room temperature in a dark place for two to three days.

Blanching

Serve green vegetables that are bright green and crisp: Plunge them into boiling water for two to three minutes, and immediately turn them into a bowl of ice water. Let stand in water only until cool, then drain. The veggies can be reheated quickly by returning them to boiling water right before serving.

OTHER TIPS

OTHER TIPS

Cooking vegetables

Brighten the flavor of frozen or canned peas, carrots, green beans, broccoli, or cauliflower by dropping a piece of lemon rind into the cooking water. You can also add 1/2 to 1 teaspoon sugar to cooked vegetables such as carrots, corn, and peas. This reduces the starchy flavors and highlights natural sweetness.

Tomato puree

Purchase a huge can of tomato puree from your local grocery warehouse club. Divide it into small amounts by filling small zippered storage bags and placing them in the freezer until needed. After one is thawed, add water to make it the consistency of tomato sauce, add salt and spices for flavor. Tomato puree contains no additives or preservatives.

Onions

Chop enough onions to fill two skillets, then saute´ them in margarine until they're translucent and slightly browned. After letting them cool, wrap portions in plastic wrap and freeze them in a large plastic bag. When you need them, just add or thaw in the microwave.

Potatoes, mashed

Make mashed potatoes ahead of time by spooning pre-prepared whipped potatoes into a buttered casserole dish. Dot with pats of butter and cover with plastic wrap and refrigerate. Before serving, bake in 350 degree oven for about 25 minutes, or until a knife inserted in the center comes out hot. Or cook in microwave until hot.

GROCERY SHOPPING

Weigh produce

Prepackaged produce must have a minimum weight as printed on the packaging. However, not all potatoes are created equal, so a 10 pound bag may weigh 11 pounds, and a one pound bag of carrots may weigh 1 1/2 pounds.

OTHER TIPS

OTHER TIPS

Cash
Grocery shop with cash only. You will be a much more careful shopper knowing you cannot go over your limit because you do not have a checkbook or credit card to fall back on. (This is particularly helpful for the compulsive shopper, who would rather stick toothpicks under her fingernails than go through the checkout only to find out she doesn't have enough money.)

Coupons
Find a market that will double the coupon's value. This practice varies throughout the country, but if you do have good coupons, make sure you find a way to double them. Some stores even triple them on certain days. Also use coupons only for items you would normally buy even if you didn't have the coupon and only if it is truly a savings. Check other brands that might be on sale or are already cheaper. Manufacturers often offer coupons as incentives on new products. But you're not saving anything if you buy something that was not on your list.

Impulse control

When you pick up an item that is not on your grocery list, place it in the child's seat of the shopping cart. Then just before checking out, reevaluate the budget-breaking items, and make yourself put all of them back except for one item. That's your reward for carefully controlling your impulses in the grocery aisles.

Spices

When purchasing spices and herbs, first check your health food store. Many carry spices and herbs in bulk quantities, and you can measure out and purchase as much or as little as you like. Don't buy more than you know you will reasonably use in the next six months.

OTHER TIPS

OTHER TIPS

Timing
Shop midweek and during off hours. Typically, store sales and double even triple coupon savings occur midweek. Also, there's less distracting hustle and bustle early or late in the day or at mealtime, which allows you to do a more efficient job of shopping.

MAKE YOUR OWN

Cafe mocha
Company's coming, and you're nearly out of coffee. Make this cafe mocha, and you can serve six people with just two cups of coffee. Add 1/3-cup cocoa and three cups warmed milk to two cups of coffee. Sweeten to taste, or add about 1/4 cup sugar.

Orange Julius™
Ingredients: two cups orange juice, 1/2 cup powdered coffee creamer, 1/2 teaspoon vanilla, two table-spoons sugar, five large ice cubes. Place ingredients in blender, add ice cubes one at a time. Blend until frothy. Yields: one to two servings.

Mousse

For a quick, cheap, and low-fat chocolate mousse: Mix cocoa powder into Cool Whip™. Add as little or as much cocoa powder as your palate dictates. Stir well and serve. Also can be used to frost cakes.

Cappuccino

To make four cappuccinos, place two cups of milk in a glass measuring cup. Microwave on high until hot, about two minutes and 20 seconds. Place hot milk and one tablespoon of sugar in a blender. Cover with a vented lid and blend until frothy, about one minute. To serve, divide two cups strong coffee among four cups. Top each with frothy milk. Sprinkle with cinnamon or grated chocolate (optional).

OTHER TIPS

OTHER TIPS

SHELF LIFE SECRETS

Bread

Loaves freeze better than slices; small amounts of bread and smaller breads such as rolls freeze best. Freeze bread uncovered until solid, then store in plastic bags. Thaw in the bag.

Cookie dough

Most unbaked cookie dough can be refrigerated for at least a week, and frozen for up to a year if it has been wrapped airtight in freezer-weight plastic bags or foil.

Eggs

Eggs will stay fresh all month in the refrigerator if you keep them on the shelf in their original cartons instead of putting them in the egg holder on the refrigerator door. The movement of the door and temperature variations from opening and closing cause eggs to spoil more quickly.

BATHROOM

Glass shower doors

Mineral oil will remove stubborn scum from the inside of glass shower doors. Give the tiles, faucets, and outside of shower door a final once-over with glass cleaner to make them really shine.

Leaking toilet

Find the water leaks. Give your home this test: Turn off all running water in the house. Find your water meter and take a look. Is it still moving? Chances are you have a water leak, and chances are even better it's your toilet. Put a few drops of food coloring into the toilet's tank. If without flushing, the color shows up in the bowl, it's leaking all right. Get a toilet repair kit at the home repair center. This is a very simple do-it-yourself repair.

Toilet cleaner

If your toilet bowl has really stubborn stains, drop one or two denture cleaning tablets into the bowl and allow to sit overnight. Brush and flush.

OTHER TIPS

OTHER TIPS

Shower curtain with water marks

Having trouble getting those filmy water spots off your shower curtain? Fill your washing machine with warm water, liquid detergent as you would for any load, and one capful of liquid fabric softener at the beginning of the wash cycle. Add fabric softener again in the rinse cycle. Your shower curtain will come out sparkling and not a water spot in sight.

Mildew

Here's a way to get rid of mildew buildup in your shower stall without using harsh, household bleach: Fill an empty spray bottle with vinegar and a cup of salt. Spray the stall, allow the solution to sit for at least a half hour, and then rinse thoroughly. Tougher jobs may require a second application.

Showerhead declogger

A showerhead that is really mired in sediment that cannot be completely removed with vinegar needs a heavy-duty treatment. Dissolve a denture-cleaning tablet in a plastic bag of water. Tie the bag over the showerhead so that it is completely immersed in the liquid. Attach with a rubberband or twist tie. Allow to sit for several hours. Remove and turn on shower to clear all traces of sediment.

DECORATING

Decorator album

Fill a purse-size photo album with paint, fabric, and wallpaper samples organized by room. Take the album when you go shopping or to garage sales, and you'll take the guesswork out of finding coordinating accessories for your home.

OTHER TIPS

OTHER TIPS

Dye to change your look

When redecorating, remember Rit™ dye. Light colored curtains, bedspreads, and throw rugs can be dyed a darker shade of another color and will give a room an entirely new look. Remember to wash these items separately in cold water. Drying in the dryer or direct sun will fade the colors quickly, so remember to allow time for air-drying indoors or in a shady place.

Hang a picture

This is a formula that professional picture hangers use: (1) Measure up 60 inches from the floor. (2) To this, add half the height of the framed picture. (3) Subtract the height of the wire (the height of the triangle that the wire would form if the frames were actually hanging in place). This magic number is the distance from the floor at which you should nail the picture hook regardless of the height of the ceiling or even your height.

Dripless candles

To make new candles dripless, soak in a strong saltwater solution for a few hours, then dry well.

Base for artificial flowers

To hold artificial flowers in place, pour salt in the container, add a little cold water, and arrange flowers. As it dries, the salt will solidify and hold the flowers.

Fresh flowers

Here's a remarkable method for greatly increasing the useful life of freshly cut flowers. Add 1/4 teaspoon of bleach to the vase water. Recut flower stems at an angle to encourage absorption and arrange them in the bleach water. Place in a cool, dark place for several hours, then put out on display. Flowers should be angle cut and refreshed daily. The bleach retards the growth of bacteria in the water, which causes flowers to wilt much more quickly.

OTHER TIPS

OTHER TIPS

Hanging on papered wall

To hang pictures on wallpaper: Cut a notch in the paper, bend it back gently, then drive the nail into the wall. If you remove the nail later, you can simply glue the paper flap over the hole, and there won't be an ugly blemish on the paper.

Candleholders

Coat the inside of a candleholder with a tiny amount of petroleum jelly to ensure easy removal.

Holiday mantelpiece

To make a gorgeous yet cheap holiday mantelpiece, lay sprays of evergreens on the mantelpiece, thread a string of white lights on green wire through them, and nestle some of your collectibles, ornaments, or pinecones amid the greens.

Table pedestal storage

Top a new trash or garbage can with a piece of plywood and cover with a floor-length fabric to turn it into a lamp table. The receptacle provides a fairly large storage space for Christmas decorations or other items used on a limited basis.

Art gallery

If you enjoy decorating your home or apartment with framed art prints, discover a wonderful resource offered by many public libraries. Some carry hundreds of framed art prints that library patrons may check out free of charge for a specified time period of two, even three months. Designate a particular wall in your home as your "revolving art gallery," where you enjoy a broad range of artistic styles at no cost to you.

Fabric paint

A touch of washable fabric paint, available at craft and fabric stores, can customize plain-Jane napkins, place mats, or tablecloths into fabulous accessories that coordinate with your dishes, floors, or wall coverings.

OTHER TIPS

OTHER TIPS

Full to queen

You don't need all new bedding if you replace your old double bed with a queen-size one. Lay a full-size flat sheet on your new queen-size mattress. Fold a hospital corner (this has a pleated rather than gathered look) at all four corners and pin them in place. Stitch elastic completely around the pleated corners. You will have a queen-size fitted sheet. Buy coordinating flat queen-size sheets when you see them on sale. Make extra pillowcases from the full-size fitted sheets.

Paneling

If you want to give a room with dark wood paneling a new look but a complete remodel is not in the budget right now, consider painting the paneling. First treat the walls with a paint deglosser. This will remove all grease, dirt, and the high gloss. Next apply a coat of white primer and follow with regular wall paint. This is a very inexpensive way to redecorate a room. Check with the paint professional at your home improvement center regarding the kind of products that would be best for this job.

Pillowcases

Pillowcases are very expensive these days, one pair can be as much as the price of a sheet, which is the reason you might want to consider making your own. When buying new sheets, pick up a fitted sheet and two flat sheets, making sure the second flat is queen-size, regardless of the size of the bed you will be outfitting. Out of the queen-size flat sheet you will be able to make three sets of pillowcases. By analyzing a commercially made pillowcase, it is easy to measure, create a pattern, and see how it is put together.

Reupholster

If you have a lovely old couch you don't want to part with, consider having it redone at an upholstery school for a fraction of a professional upholsterer's price. There is a fee, and advanced students typically charge $100.00. You'll be expected to purchase fabric through the school. Plan on students taking a little longer to complete the job, whose work is done under the supervision of teachers. Look under "Upholstery Schools" in your Yellow Pages™ or call the industrial arts divisions of high schools and colleges.

OTHER TIPS

OTHER TIPS

Wide curtain rods

Current home decorating styles often include window valances that are hung on two 1/2 inch rods rather than the typical skinny ones. If you don't want to spend money to get the wider ones, you can update your skinny rods. Cut two 1/2 inch strips of wood from an old piece of paneling and use a hot glue gun to attach the strips to the skinny rod. Attach to the existing hardware, which should still be in place on the wall. New valances can be slipped right over the rod.

GARDENING

Club soda

Don't throw away your fizzless club soda. It has just the right chemicals to add vigor and beautiful color to most house plants. Use it as you would water to hydrate the plant.

Plant with a purpose

Plant deciduous trees (the type that lose their leaves in winter) on the south side of your house. They will provide summer shade without blocking winter sun. Plant evergreens on the north to shield your home from cold winter winds.

Master gardener

Most states offer gardening programs through their county extension offices. Gardening experts teach enrollees all aspects of gardening. Typically there are no fees; however, "students" are required to donate time to the community in trade for the education. Call your local directory assistance for the office nearest you.

Plant nutrition

Don't throw out the water in which you've boiled eggs or pasta. The calcium and starches are great for watering houseplants.

Rabbits away

Sprinkle red pepper or talcum powder around the base of plants to keep rabbits away.

OTHER TIPS

OTHER TIPS

Water

Gardens need an inch of water a week. But how do you know how long to water to achieve that goal? Place a can, pot, or glass under your sprinkler and see how long it takes for the container to collect an inch of water. Once you have this information, install automatic timers on your watering systems. Watering less often for a longer period of time allows deep penetration and reduces the total amount of water consumed.

Wick while away

If you must leave small potted plants unattended while on vacation, push a needle threaded with wool yarn into the soil, and put the other end in a jar of water. The plants will stay moist through this wicking system.

Ants

Follow the ants' trail to their point of entry into the house and seal it with caulk. Then find their nest (at the other end of their trail) and destroy it by pouring several gallons of boiling water into the entrance, stir it up, and pour more boiling water.

Ashes

Ashes from a wood burning stove or fireplace make wonderful fertilizer for rose bushes and other prizes in your yard and garden. Collect the ashes, and scatter them around shrubs and bushes. Ashes enrich the soil's texture and will produce a greener garden. Fireplace ashes act like lime in the garden, making your soil more alkaline. If your soil is already alkaline, you don't need to use them. A gallon of dry ashes equals about three pounds and if used as a soil additive, apply at the rate of five pounds per 100 square feet.

Bug detector

If you are concerned about bringing in bugs along with your just-picked produce, rinse garden-fresh vegetables well, then let soak in mixture of one gallon water and one cup vinegar for about five minutes. Insects will be easier to pick off and your produce's flavor will not be affected.

Cut early

The best time to cut flowers is in the early morning while they retain some moisture from the cool night air and the early-morning dew.

OTHER TIPS

OTHER TIPS

Cheap sod

If you have more time than money and need a new lawn, visit your local sod farm and purchase their "scraps," which are the odd-sized roll ends. You will have to patch it together which takes time, but you can pick up these odd pieces at a tremendous savings.

Florist prepared plants

When you receive live floral plants in those beautiful wrapped containers, the wrapping material may become deadly to the plant. The pot in which the plant is planted has holes at the bottom, but the foil or plastic wrapping prevents drainage. To eliminate this problem hold the container high, punch a hole in the center, tear outward, and with scissors carefully cut all around to within an inch or so of the edge. The overall appearance is left undisturbed and the plant can drain properly and will be able to thrive.

Photograph your hard work

Use up the last few frames on a roll of film to photograph your garden in bloom. This is a great way to keep a record of what grew well and what plantings you particularly enjoyed.

Gardener hands

Two ways to remove garden soil from your hands and from beneath your fingernails: (1) Soak your hands in water in which one of those fizzy denture-cleaning tablets has dissolved. An added bonus: soft cuticles. (2) After a day of gardening, wash your hands with soap and water and a teaspoon of regular table sugar. The rough granules will scour your hands clean.

Weed killer

Here's a great weed killer you can make for less than $2.00 a gallon. Dissolve one pound table salt in one gallon white vinegar (five percent acidity is ideal). Add eight drops of liquid dishwashing detergent (helps plant material absorb the liquid). Label and keep out of reach of children. Use in an ordinary spray bottle. This non-toxic formulation acts as a temporary soil sterilizer, so don't spray near roots of trees, shrubs, or plants you'd like to keep. I find it especially effective on my gravel driveway.

OTHER TIPS

OTHER TIPS

HOUSEKEEPING

Air conditioner location

If you have an option, install window air conditioners in north and east facing windows. South and west facing windows receive more sun and will make the unit work harder.

Carpet bargain

If you are not in a big hurry and are fairly flexible as to color and quality, let the carpet store in your area that offer "Complete Satisfaction Guaranteed" know that you would be interested in purchasing the carpeting someone else rejected. Many times when new carpet is installed, the homeowner for one reason or another is not completely satisfied with some aspect of the carpet and takes advantage of the carpet supplier's satisfaction guarantee. You should be able to make a real bargain on the like-new goods, including installation.

Relaxing wallpaper

If vinyl wallpaper is too tightly curled, you can relax it with a hair dryer set on warm. Hold the dryer six to eight inches away, and wave it back and forth over the paper.

Clogged drain

If a drain is completely stopped up, don't try to clear it with chemical drain cleaners. They may bubble back up into the sink or tub and cause permanent damage to the finish of the fixture. If there's only a moderate clog, pour boiling water with a few teaspoons of ammonia down the drain, wait a few minutes, then plunge.

Cubbies

Here's an uplifting idea: Don't forget to look up for extra storage. A row of cubbies (storage boxes) attached to the wall over coat hooks is one example of found space. Other logical locations are above a washer or dryer, chest of drawers, medicine cabinet, or window.

OTHER TIPS

OTHER TIPS

Glue it up

Almost anything can be attached to a wall with a hot-glue gun. When you want to move it or simply reposition, a few seconds from your hair dryer will reheat the glue, soften it, and then you can move it easily. The best part? No more unsightly nail holes. (Test this first inside a closet, and use common sense in determining how much weight to hang with this method.)

Nails, screws, and heat

To keep the wall or plaster from splitting or cracking when hammering in a nail, drip the nail into a pot of hot water for 15 seconds, then carefully hammer it in. To remove a stubborn screw, pass a lighted match over the end of the screwdriver; the hot tip will then twist out the screw.

Freezer

Be sure to keep your freezer packed full to consume the least amount of energy. As your store of food is depleted, fill the gaps with plastic jugs filled with water. You'll accomplish a keep-it-full technique and have a good supply of fresh water in the event of a power failure.

Refinish ceramic tile

If your kitchen or bathroom is suffering from outdated avocado green or some other 1970's colored ceramic tile, and you don't choose to replace it at this time, do this: Purchase a product like Fleckstone™ (manufactured by Plasti-kote™), available at home improvement centers. It is a multihued, textured spray paint sold together with a clear acrylic topcoat that, when applied as directed, produces "new" tile that can be cleaned with a damp sponge. Even if it takes five kits to do the job, you'll spend around $50.00 and that sure beats remodeling.

Cheapest clothes dryer

Gas dryers are so much cheaper to operate than electric ones that under typical circumstances you will recoup the higher purchase cost of about $100.00 in a year. Electric dryers perform slightly better than gas, but the lower cost of gas more than compensates for these minor differences. If you get a gas dryer, buy one with an electronic ignition. A dryer with a pilot light uses 30 percent more gas and will increase your fuel bill by about $25.00 a year.

OTHER TIPS

OTHER TIPS

Refrigerators

Manual defrost refrigerators typically use about half as much electricity as automatic defrost models, but if you don't keep up with the defrosting, the refrigerator's efficiency will drop. Side-by-side refrigerator/freezers typically use 35 percent more energy than models with the freezer on top.

Leave it on

Computers don't like being turned on. The chance of failure during that time is high enough that many businesses never turn off their machines. If you step away from the computer and intend to return within three or four hours, leave it on. However, if you do not have a screen saver, turn the monitor off to avoid burning images into the display. Every monitor has its own on-off switch.

Warranty book

Save receipts, warranties, and owner's manuals. Often these are all you will need to have an appliance repaired at no charge. Find a three-ring binder fitted with plastic pocket protectors to keep everything neat and orderly.

Audit long-distance bills

Have your phone bill audited by several long-distance providers. Some long-distance companies offer auditing services at no charge. You send them several monthly bills, and they determine what you would have paid had you used their service. If you decide to switch, make sure all fees to make the move will be waived and that you can go back if you are unsatisfied with the new service.

Baking soda

Baking soda is a nonabrasive cleanser. Use it without worry on fine china, porcelain appliances, the inside of the refrigerator, stainless steel, aluminum, and cast iron. You can use it either in its powdered form or mix it with water to make a paste. Baking soda is a wonderful cleanser for everything from countertops to rolling pins to gold-trimmed dishes. If you want to remove an offensive odor, think baking soda.

Grease marks on wallpaper

Remove a grease spot from wallpaper by rubbing baby powder into it. This serves as an absorbent.

OTHER TIPS

OTHER TIPS

Check for deposits

Usually if you have been a good customer of the utility companies (gas, water, electricity, phone) for at least a year, you can arrange to have your deposits refunded or credited toward your account. You may be able to get interest, too, if you ask.

Drain maintenance

To clear a sluggish drain, pour one cup baking soda into the drain followed by one cup white vinegar. Allow to sit overnight. In the morning flush with a kettle full of boiling water. Plunge the drain a few times with a plunger. This is an excellent maintenance tactic to keep drains running well.

Drawer organizer

Keep your earrings, small bracelets, and necklaces in the separate compartments of a plastic ice tray. The tray fits in a dresser drawer so jewels stay neat and out of sight.

Home energy audits

Request a home energy audit from your electricity and gas companies. Typically these audits are free and will help you discover where all that energy is leaking out of the house.

Drill a water leak

If you notice water leaking through the ceiling, immediately hammer a 16d nail through the sheetrock to allow the water to drain before it damages the plaster or drywall. Later, after the leak is repaired, all you'll need to cover the emergency repair is a dab of Spackle™ and touch-up paint.

Move midweek

If you're moving, do it on a weekday. Fees can be as much as 50 percent higher on the weekend. Pack everything yourself and save at least 10 percent. Most movers provide cartons.

Moving boxes

Before you tape a box shut, run a piece of string along the path where you'll be placing the tape. Press the tape over the string to seal the box, leaving a bit of string hanging loose. When it's time to unpack, just pull on the string to rip the tape.

OTHER TIPS

OTHER TIPS

Moving to a new home

If you have a wall arrangement you are particularly fond of or a furniture arrangement that works particularly well, photograph it to use as a reference when you rehang and resettle everything in your new home.

Dryer sheets

Save the dryer sheets from your laundry after they've softened a load of wash. They make great dusting and cleaning cloths for television and computer screens. Not only will they clean the screens, the antistatic properties will treat the screens to repel rather than attract dust.

Reference information

When you finish refurbishing a room in your home, write down this important information on a piece of paper and tape it to the back of the switch plate: the brand and color of the paint, how much it took to paint the room, how many rolls of wallpaper were required, and the circuit breaker number that serves this room. You'll be happy to find the information the next time.

BANKING

Checks direct
Don't buy checks from the bank. You can save 50 percent of what they charge by ordering through an independent source like Current, 800-426-0822, or Checks-in-the-Mail, 800-733-4443.

Credit unions
Many credit unions offer low or no fee checking accounts and free checks too. If there's any way you can qualify, join a credit union. Most credit unions welcome spouses, children, brothers, sisters, and parents of the member. You will enjoy federally-insured deposits and low interest auto loans. And you'll earn higher than bank interest rates on your savings accounts.

OTHER TIPS

OTHER TIPS

Personal identification numbers (PIN)

Never write your PIN number on your debit or credit card or on anything that would readily identify what it is. Instead "embed" it in a phone number under a fictitious entry in your phone book. Example: If your PIN number is 3614, make an entry of "Penelope 361-4000." Choose a PIN that can't be traced, and never select a number that can be derived from the contents of your wallet.

ATM safety

When using the automatic teller machine, always wait for the "Welcome" prompt to signal that your transaction is over, and then take your card. Leaving prematurely may allow the next customer to continue making transactions in your account.

Shop around

Switch to a smaller, locally owned bank. The fee structure will likely be lower and some services will actually be offered at no cost, such as free checking, free checks, etc.

Automatic banking

Arrange with your bank or credit union to have your paycheck automatically deposited, your bills paid automatically, and your savings funded automatically from your checking account. With this type of arrangement you will be handling your money less so you won't be so tempted to play games with the account. The typical bank charge is about $7.00 a month to handle one's money in this way-quite a bargain; at least half of that would be paid in postage alone. Your bank will be able to answer all of your questions.

CREDIT CARDS

You have to ask

If you receive a new credit card with a remarkably lower interest rate, call your current credit card company and tell them about this competing offer. If you have a good track record with them, and they get the message that you just might leave in favor of the more attractive rate, you could receive an on-the-spot interest rate reduction. You'll wonder why you didn't call sooner.

OTHER TIPS

OTHER TIPS

Credit card applications

One of the problems of paying off credit card debt and cleaning up one's credit rating is the number of pre-approved credit card offers that begin arriving in the mail. In order to stop these offers write to: Equifax Options, P.O. Box 740123, Atlanta, GA 30374-0123. Include your complete name, full address, social security number, and signature. Equifax is one of the three major credit reporting agencies. They will remove your name from the lists they provide and will also share your request with the other two agencies, Experian and TransUnion.

Annual fees

Credit card companies deny publicly that they waive annual fees, but insiders admit the practice is often used to save valuable customers. Squawk and you shall receive.

HOMEOWNERS TIPS

Buying a bargain property

If you're looking for a bargain, buy the worst house in a good neighborhood. You can always fix up a house, but you can't change the neighborhood.

Interest on earnest money

When purchasing a home, make sure you will earn interest on your deposit during the escrow period.

Homeowner's insurance

Ask about homeowner's insurance discounts for security systems, smoke alarms, and good driving records. Always ask! The agent or company may not volunteer the information.

Property taxes

Challenge your property tax bill. If the value of your property has declined, you might be entitled to a reassessment of your taxes.

Mortgage interest rate

Inquire if the financial institution servicing your mortgage offers an interest rate reduction when payments are automatically paid from your checking account. Example: A credit union recently introduced a 1/4 percent reduction for any member who authorizes automatic withdrawal.

OTHER TIPS

OTHER TIPS

Principal prepayments

Instead of paying your mortgage monthly, pay half of your mortgage payment every two weeks. You will end up making 26 half-payments, which equal 13 monthly payments. Your spending plan will absorb this additional payment with little, if any, pain, and your principal will love you. If your mortgage holder will not accept payments in this way, make your regular monthly payment as required, and include a second check equal to 1/12 of one payment. At year-end you will have made the equivalent of 13 monthly payment with the same effect. Simply write "Principal prepayment" on the second check.

Negotiating trick

When negotiating the purchase or sale of a home, always ask for more than you are willing to accept-even if that is beyond your level of expectation, and you're sure they'd never agree. More than likely your opponent will meet you halfway, in essence splitting the difference. That's what makes both of you winners. You get more than you ever dreamed possible, and they didn't have to give nearly as much as they thought you expected. It's called the "art of negotiation."

MONEY SAVING TIPS

Hope they won't be undersold

Even though the store where you made a recent purchase doesn't advertise a "we won't be undersold" policy, always take a chance. If, say, the day after you make the purchase, you notice a sale by their competitor during which the same item is offered at 50 percent off, take your purchase back, along with the competitor's ad, and simply ask what they can do for you. You'll be surprised what companies will do to keep a customer.

OTHER TIPS

OTHER TIPS

Customer service documentation

When requesting a refund, repair, or replacement, keep track of all communications on a calendar. Summarize phone calls and send a follow-up letter of understanding. Don't give up until you are satisfied.

IRA contribution

Try to contribute to your individual retirement account (IRA) as early in the year as possible. The difference between making your contributions each January 1 rather than December 31 of the same year can spell thousands of dollars of additional earnings in your account over the decades.

Renter's insurance

If you rent, buy a tenant's policy. This is a must. Landlords are not responsible for your belongings in case of disaster.

Know what you have

Call the Social Security Administration at 800-772-1213 for a "Request for Earnings and Benefits Estimate Statement." After you mail back the completed form, you will receive a statement showing all the money you have paid into social security as well as a personalized estimated monthly benefit upon retirement. If there are errors, such as they didn't credit you one year or they have you earning the wrong amount, they can be corrected but only if you report them.

Make savings a regular bill

Once a month, or whenever you pay your bills, write a check to deposit in your money market fund or your savings account. If you can't start with 10 percent, start with less and increase the amount each month. Use automatic savings plans; let the bank take your savings out of your paycheck. You won't miss what you don't see.

Pay annually

If possible, pay insurance premiums annually. Avoid the added costs for monthly or quarterly billing.

OTHER TIPS

OTHER TIPS

Call first

If you have a consumer problem save time by calling first and ask to speak to the service desk or manager. Explain your problem and then inquire what their procedure is for fast and effective resolution. If this is not satisfactory, have a clear idea of exactly how you would like the matter resolved.

Grace period

Credit card interest is a terrible waste of money. Pay you bill in full every month during the grace period. If your credit card company charges a penalty or fee for not carrying a balance, cancel that card. There are plenty of no fee companies who will be happy to have your business.

Customer service documentation

When requesting a refund, repair, or replacement, keep track of all communications on a calendar. Summarize phone calls and send a follow-up letter of understanding. Don't give up until you are satisfied.

Warranties

Find a large three-ring binder and a supply of plastic pocket inserts. Whenever you purchase a product, whether it's appliance, lawn tool, or toy, staple the receipt to the owner's manual or warranty paperwork and file it away in one of the pockets. Now whenever something stops working or has a problem, you'll have the paperwork and all the information at your fingertips, including the customer service number. Always call, even if the warranty is expired, explain the situation, your purchase details, and then ask one simple question: What can you do for me?

Pay early in the month

Make credit card payments as early in the billing month as possible or make two smaller payments a month if you can't pay it all early. Most banks calculate interest on the average daily balance. The larger the payment and the sooner in the month you make it the more of it will apply to the principal. It may not be much savings at first, perhaps a buck or two, but savings grow month after month until the card is paid off.

OTHER TIPS

OTHER TIPS

Save creatively

If you find yourself borrowing back the money you've determined to save, here are some tips for how to put some space between you and the stash: (1) Keep your savings and checking accounts in different banks. (2) Open a passbook account, which will limit your access to the funds. (3) Open your savings account in a bank in another city and make all of your deposits by mail. (4) Establish an account that requires two signatures to withdraw.

Auto savings

Make arrangements with your employer to automatically deposit a certain percentage of your paycheck directly into your savings account and the balance into your checking. What you don't see you won't miss, and this is the most painless way to start saving.

Guidelines for beginning investors

As a beginning investor, any plan you consider should have all the following features or you run a great risk of failure: (1) The investment must be simple to understand and easy to follow. (2) It must take very little time to administrate. (3) It should not cause you stress or anxiety. (4) It must not change your lifestyle or cause disharmony in your home. (5) You must be able to handle the investment entirely on your own. (6) It must have the advantage of liquidity (getting your money back quickly in the event of an emergency). (7) It must work equally well for the person with very little to invest as well as the wealthy investor.

U.S. savings bonds

Here's how to earn double interest. Buy U.S. Series EE Savings Bonds on the last day of the month with money that has been earning interest in another account during the month. The bond starts accruing interest as if purchased on the first day of the month. Example: Buy a bond on June 30. When you receive the bond about 21 days later, it will be recorded as of June 1.

OTHER TIPS

OTHER TIPS

Health insurance

Shop your health insurance coverage regularly. With many companies the first year premium is much less, so switching may not be a bad idea. If your employer offers a menu of coverages, check them all carefully and determine which is best for your particular situation. Never cancel one coverage until you have another fully in place.

Rate reduction

Be sure to let your auto insurance company know of any changes to your driving record, such as if you have been driving to work but have recently joined a car pool, or have been commuting but quit your job to stay at home. Both of these events would result in a significant rate reduction.

Bill-paying routine

Get into the habit of paying bills twice each month, say, on the first and fifteenth. During the month as the bills arrive, follow this routine: Open a bill and place the return envelope and throw the rest away. Write the due date on the outside of the envelope and separate into two due-date piles: "1st of the month" and "15th of the month."

Life motto

Stop spending money you do not have in your possession today. That means no charging on credit cards, no borrowing from friends or relatives. If that sounds too radical and impossible, agree to not incur any debt just for today. Taking it one day at a time is really much easier.

Start saving for the future

Regardless of how much in debt you are or how little money you make, saving something consistently in a special place or account is going to change your attitude. Saving even a few dollars each week helps fill the emptiness that drives some of us to spend. Something of everything you earn is yours to keep.

OTHER TIPS

OTHER TIPS

Coupon stash

Many banks are opening convenient branch offices in major grocery stores. If this is true for the supermarket you frequent, open a savings account. Now when you buy groceries, write your check for the total before coupons are subtracted. Ask for your coupon savings back in cash (the equivalent of writing a check for more than the purchase amount), and make a deposit to your savings account on your way out with that cash. Also, make a point of writing your check for more than the purchase by $5.00 to $10.00 if your can manage. Stash that cash into the bank as you leave, as well. It's a painless and convenient way to save.

AUTOMOBILE BUYING

Dealer add-ons

Factory-installed options are good buys, but think twice about any option the dealer wants to add, such as a stereo or sunroof. Typically, specialty shops do better work and charge half the price.

Automobile twins

Even if you have your heart set on a particular vehicle, remember that many cars have twins. General Motors offers many of the same cars as Chevrolets, Buicks, Pontiacs, or Oldsmobiles. Chrysler often clones its cars as Dodges and Plymouths. The Geo Prism is essentially a Toyota Corolla built in the U.S., while the Ford Probe and Mazda MX-6 are twins. The annual car issue of *Consumer Reports* tells you which automobiles are twins.

Dealers' fiscal year

If you are in the market to buy a new car, wait until the end of March. December is not the end of most dealers' fiscal year as most would like you to believe, but March is.

OTHER TIPS

OTHER TIPS

Buyer's guide sticker

If you are considering buying a used car from a dealer, become familiar with the Buyer's Guide sticker posted on every used car offered for sale (for-sale-by-owner cars excluded). It was originated by the Federal Trade Commission as a consumer protection device. Before you start shopping, read the FTC pamphlet that explains the Buyer's Guide. Send 50 cents to : Consumer Information Center-F, P.O. Box 100, Pueblo, CO 81002, and request publication 440T "Buying a Used Car."

Research prices for 30 days

Before you shop for a used car, be it from a dealer or private seller, know the general value of cars you're shopping for. Study a month's worth of classified ads to learn what your dream car goes for on the private market.

New car test

When you finally take a new car home, give it a long and thorough test-drive. Take the car back immediately if you detect a major problem. The courts have upheld demands for a refund when the car was returned within the first few days.

AUTOMOBILE CARE

Battery terminals

Pour club soda on the battery terminals. It's a great way to quickly clean and neutralize the acid residue at the battery terminals. In a pinch, even a cola will do.

Coolant, always

Always keep a mix of equal parts antifreeze and water in your car's cooling system, even if you live in a mild climate where it never freezes. Not only will it keep your cooling system functioning well, antifreeze contains valuable rust inhibitors.

Correct gasoline is best

Make sure you use the octane grade gasoline recommended in your car's owner's manual. Using a more expensive higher-octane gas than recommended will deliver no benefit, and a lower-octane gas than recommended could damage the engine.

Oil bargains

Stockpile oil, oil filters, and air filters when they go on sale. Unopened bottles of oil don't have a shelf life problem.

OTHER TIPS

OTHER TIPS

Drain and replace

Drain and replace your car's radiator fluid every other year. The anticorrosion elements of coolant are spent in about two years.

Dealer parts

As a rule, car dealers go for greed and charge 30 to 70 percent more for auto parts than auto-parts stores do. Make a habit of checking auto parts stores first before running to the dealer. And don't overlook the auto wrecking yards. They're the best deal going if you don't need a new part. Unfortunately, many parts are available only through the dealer, so in some situations you're stuck.

Emergency fan belt

Pantyhose can come through as an emergency fan belt if your car fan breaks. Cut the panty portion away and twirl both legs into a rope; wrap the strong nylon rope around your car engine pulleys; make two knots and cut off the loose end. Start your car and drive slowly for several miles to a gas station or telephone.

Radial tires

When buying tires, choose radials over bias-ply. You'll pay more up front but will save in the long run. Radials deliver better mileage because they have less rolling resistance. More importantly, they last 15 to 20 percent longer.

Secret warranties

Some automakers issue special warranties on certain aspects of the auto that are kept quiet and secret from the automobile owner. To find out if your car has secret warranties, send the year, make, and model along with a large self-addressed, stamped envelope to the Center for Auto Safety, 2001 S Street NW, Washington, DC 20009. They will respond with a description of all secret warranties on your car.

OTHER TIPS

OTHER TIPS

Auto gadget caddy

A large handbag or other kind of handled tote with its many zippered compartments makes a dandy storage system for the trunk of your car. Fill the pockets with battery cables, flashlight, first aid kit, maps, window cleaner, paper towels, and a plastic window scraper.

Snow chains caddy

Start with an old pair of jeans. Cut off the legs to make short shorts. Sew the legs shut. Drop one chain into each "leg" compartment, and the tools required for installation fit easily into the pockets. Attach handles for easy carrying.

AIRLINE TRAVEL

Travel size

Save 35mm film containers for holding face cream, laundry detergent, and other travel supplies you need in small quantities while traveling.

Fare wars

If you purchase an airline ticket and before you use it the airlines have a big fare war, you may be able to receive the difference. Check with your airline for the specific rules and regulations, and don't wait for them to call you. They won't.

Rebooking shortcut

You're at the airport when you learn, that your flight has been canceled. Don't rush to the ticket counter where you will wait in line with everyone else on the canceled flight. Instead find a phone and call the airline's reservation number. Ask to be rebooked on the next scheduled flight.

Rule 240

If your flight is delayed due to mechanical or scheduling problems, don't fret. Rule 240 requires most airlines to put you on another flight if it can get you there sooner than the flight they have picked out for you, even if the flight is with a different airline. A copy of Rule 240 is available at every airline gate. If the employees are hesitant to grant your request, mention Rule 240 and things should change dramatically.

OTHER TIPS

OTHER TIPS

Travel iron

A hair dryer can double as a travel iron. Dampen the creased garment and spread it on a flat surface. Set the dryer on warm and hold it in one hand while smoothing the item with the other.

Back-to-Back booking

Since flights that involve weekend stays are less expensive than those that don't, on some routes it's cheaper to buy two round-trip tickets and throw away half of each.

Reduce delays

When booking a flight, remember that the more times you land, take off, or change planes the more you increase the chance of delays. If you cannot avoid making connections, look for a flight that has stopovers at small airports. Reduced traffic reduces delays. Allow at least an hour for connections.